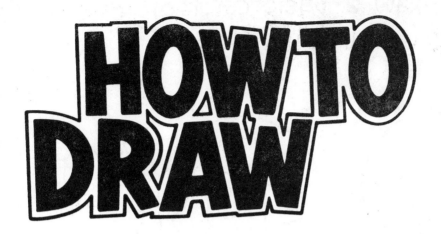

HOW TO DRAW

Not everyone is an artist. . .but almost anyone can learn to draw by following step-by-step instructions. If you can draw a fairly good circle freehand (you can practice first!), you can draw the characters in this book. And with lots of experience, who knows? You may become an artist after all.

You will need a good drawing surface. Use strong paper with a slightly rough surface (like the paper in this book). Pencils slip on a surface which is shiny; erasers make holes in paper that is too thin.

Pencils with medium-soft lead work the best (e.g. No. 2). Have a pencil sharpener handy to keep points sharp. A ruler will help you draw straight lines. Be sure to have a good eraser. Add a good light source and you're ready to begin.

Circles, ovals and pears are shapes used most often in drawing. Lines for neck, arms and legs form a simple skeleton to hold the shapes together. Always start drawings by *lightly* sketching the basic shapes.

Now let's get started. You can work right in this book on the spaces provided on each page. There are extra blank pages in the back of the book for more practice. Have fun!

to DRAW a Basic CARTOON HEAD, BEGiN WiTH SiMPLe SHaPes.

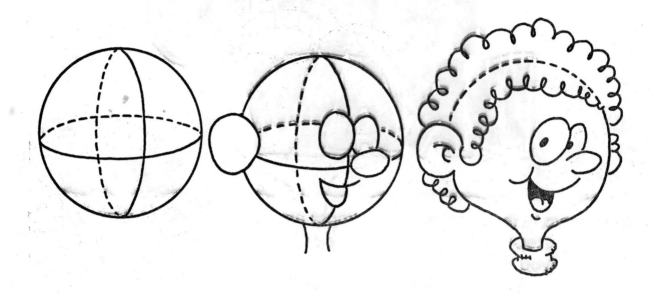

aDD DeTails to COMPLete YOUR DRaWiNG.

WITH DIFFERENT DETAILS, YOU CAN CREATE
NEW CHARACTERS.

TRY DRAWING SOME DIFFERENT EXPRESSIONS.

SURPRISED

ANGRY

HAPPY

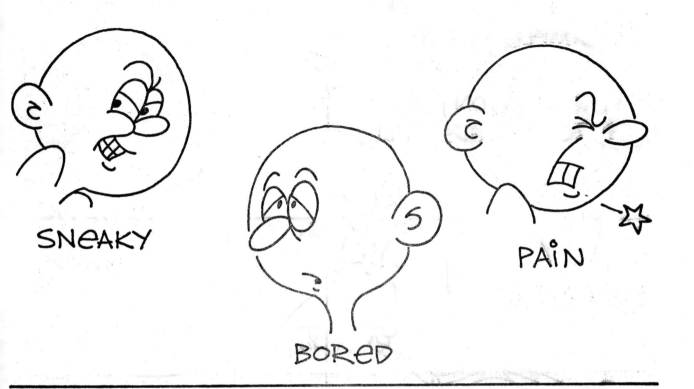

SNEAKY

BORED

PAIN

the COMIC FiGURe is
also made UP OF
SiMPLe SHaPes.

the CaRTOON MaN is
tHRee "HeaDS" TaLL.

1.

2.

3.

1.

2.

3.

BY ADDING DETAILS,
YOU CAN CREATE
ALMOST ANY
CHARACTER
YOU WANT.

1.

2.

3.

1.

2.

3.

HOW'S THIS
FOR A
BASKETBALL
STAR?

TRY A FEW
ACTION FIGURES.

PUT DIFFERENT COSTUMES AND DETAILS ON YOUR CHARACTERS...

AND LIKE MAGIC, A DIFFERENT CHARACTER WILL APPEAR.

MORE COSTUMES

THE CARTOON WOMAN
IS CONSTRUCTED
SIMILARLY TO
THE CARTOON MAN.

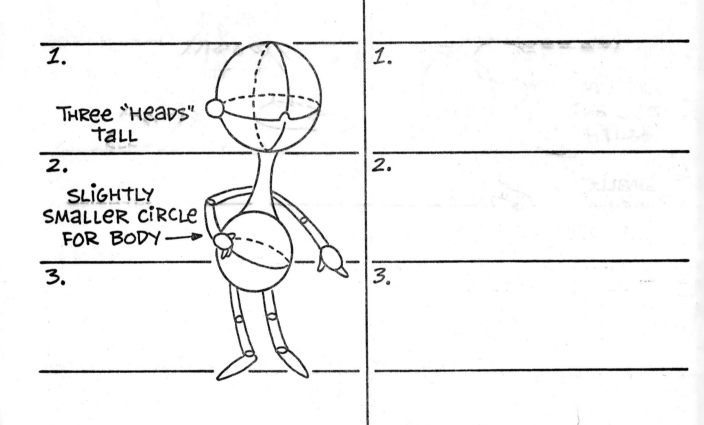

1.

THREE "HEADS"
TALL

2.

SLIGHTLY
SMALLER CIRCLE
FOR BODY →

3.

1.

2.

3.

THE CARTOON WOMAN'S
GESTURES ARE MORE
GRACEFUL THAN THE
CARTOON MAN'S.

1.

SMALLER
NOSE AND
MOUTH

2.

SMALLER
HANDS
AND FEET

3.

1.

2.

3.

HeRe aRe some
WOmeN iN
DiFFeReNT
COsTUmes.

NOTICE THAT HAIR STYLES GIVE DIFFERENT LOOKS.

CHILDReN aRe 2½ "HeaDs" TaLL.

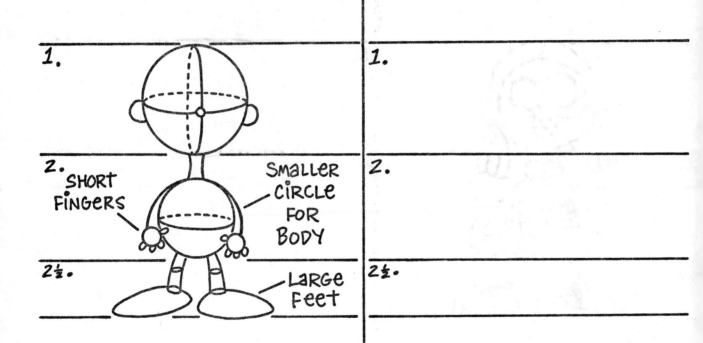

1.

2. SHORT FINGeRS

SMALLeR CiRCLe FOR BODY

2½.

LaRGe FeeT

1.

2.

2½.

HERE is a little CARTOON GiRL...

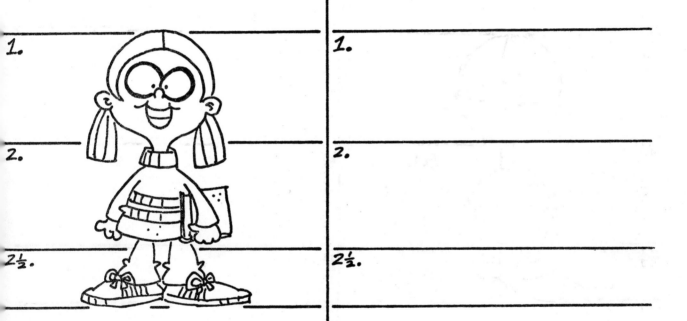

1.

1.

2.

2.

2½.

2½.

...and here is a
little cartoon boy.

1.

1.

2.

2.

2½.

2½.

CAN YOU DRAW THESE BOYS AND GIRLS?

THE CARTOON BABY'S HEAD IS MADE UP
OF A CIRCLE CONNECTED TO AN OVAL.

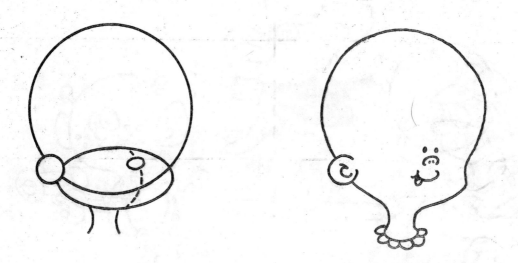

THE BABY'S FEATURES ARE TINY.

the CARTOON BABY'S
HEAD is LARGER
THAN THE CiRCLE
USED FOR iT'S BODY.

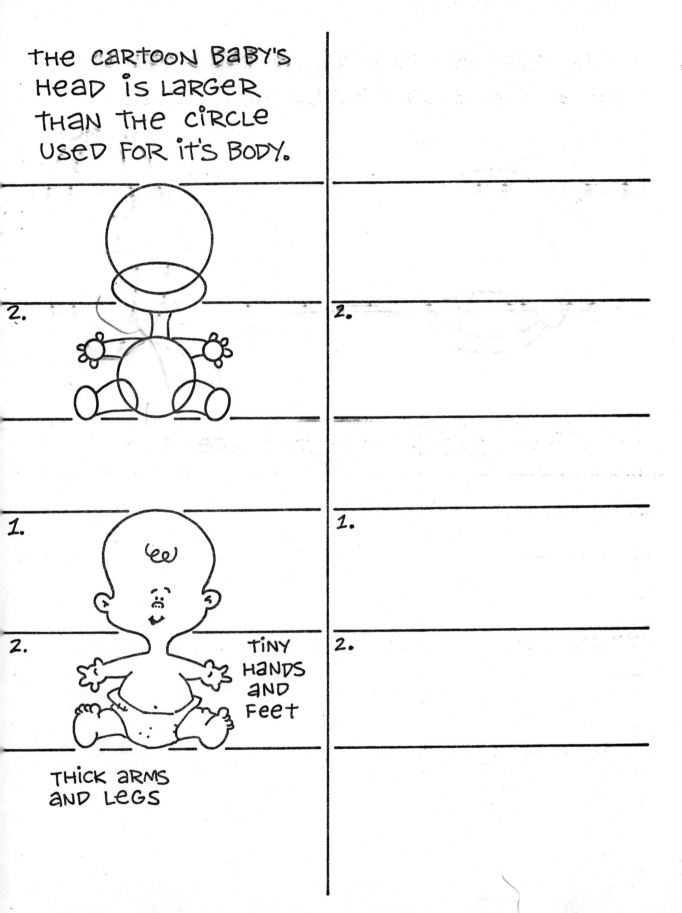

2.

2.

1.

1.

2.

TiNY
HaNDS
AND
FEET

2.

THICK ARMS
AND LEGS

YOU CAN MAKE CARTOON FACES OUT OF
ALMOST ANY SHAPE.

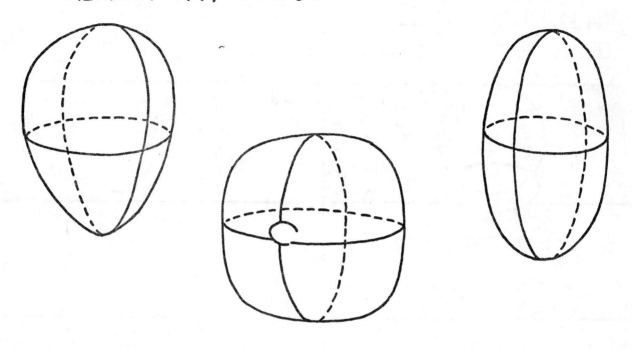

NOW GIVE iT A TRY iN THE SPACE BELOW.

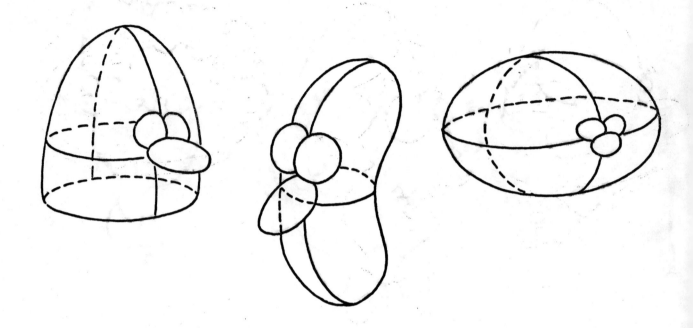

TRY TO MAKE THESE FACES FROM THE SHAPES ON THE OPPOSITE PAGE.

TO DRAW A FAT PERSON, START WITH A LARGE OVAL FOR THE BODY AND A SMALL CIRCLE FOR THE HEAD.

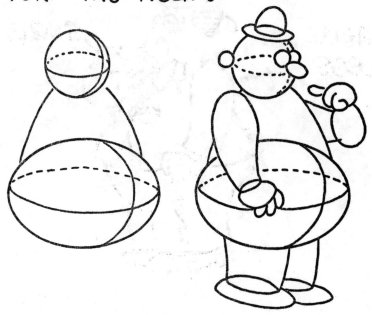

THE FAT PERSON

THICK ARMS
AND LEGS

SMALL HANDS

TO DRAW A SKINNY PERSON, START WITH A TUBE FOR THE BODY AND A THIN OVAL FOR THE HEAD.

THE SKINNY PERSON

LONG, THIN
ARMS AND LEGS.

BIG FEET

HERE'S a COLLECTION OF PEOPLE in all SHAPES AND SIZES.

1. _____

2. _____

3. _____

1. _____

2. _____

3. _____

1. _____

2. _____

3. _____

1. _____

2. _____

3. _____

DRAWING IS FUN AND EASY. ALL IT TAKES IS PRACTICE!

PRACTICE PAGES